WHITE HOUSE

Kelly White & Diane Lindsey Reeves

Created and produced by
Bright Futures Press, Cary, North Carolina
www.brightfuturespress.com

Published by
Cherry Lake Publishing, Ann Arbor, Michigan
www.cherrylakepublishing.com

Editorial Contributions by Kim Childress

Photo Credits: cover, Shutterstock/Tupungato; page 5, Shutterstock/TATSIANAMA; page 5, Shutterstock/brandonht; page 5, Shutterstock/Joseph Sohm; page 7, Flickr/White House Photostream; page 9, Shutterstock/Andrey_Popov; page 9, Shutterstock/a studio; page 11, Shutterstock/bibiphoto; page 13, Shutterstock/Orhan Cam; page 13, topvectors.com; page 15, Flickr/White House Photostream; page 17, Shutterstock/wellphoto; page 17, Shutterstock/fotoscool; page 19, Shutterstock/Picsfive; page 21, Shutterstock/David Stuart Productions; page 21, Shutterstock/alexskopje; page 23, Shutterstock/LouLou Photos; page 25, Shutterstock/Scott Rothstein; page 25, Shutterstock/C12; page 27, Flickr/White House Photostream; page 29, Shutterstock/Sean Pavone; page 29, Shutterstock/Africa Photo.

Library of Congress Cataloging-in-Publication Date

CIP has been filed and is available at catalog.loc.gov.

Printed in the United States of America.

WHITE HOUSE

Home of the free. Land of the brave.

Welcome to the nation's capital in Washington, D.C. This is where the three branches of the federal government—executive, legislative and judicial—are headquartered. It is also where the president lives with his or her family and works with hundreds of staff members at the White House. History is made here every day!

Our first president, George Washington, chose the site where the White House is located but he was the only U.S. president who didn't get to live there. The White House has 132 rooms, 35 bathrooms, and 6 levels. There are also 412 doors, 147 windows, 28 fireplaces, 8 staircases, and 3 elevators. It is a big house where BIG things happen!

The president needs lots of help to run a nation. People with many different kinds of skills and professions work in the White House to get the job done.

What if you could work in the White House someday? Would you want to be president or an important advisor? Would you want to plan important events or protect the president's family? Read on to choose your very own White House career adventure!

TABLE OF CONTENTS

CHIEF USHER

Ready to take charge of running the president's house? Looking for an energetic, extremely organized individual interested in long-term commitment to manage the household staff and behind-the-scenes operations of the White House. Awesome organizational skills a must and budgetary know-how a very big plus. Here's your chance to leave a mark on history!

- *Ready to take on this challenge?*
  Turn to page 6.

- *Want to explore a career as an Intelligence Officer instead?*
  Go to page 9.

- *Rather consider other choices?*
  Return to page 4.

Learn more about what the chief usher does at www.whitehousehistory. org/questions/who-is-the-chief-usher.

Work at Home

The White House is where the United States of America does business! But the White House is also home to the presidential family. A staff of hundreds work there every day including maids, chefs, butlers, florists, doormen, painters, plumbers, carpenters, electricians, gardeners, and many more. As **chief usher**, you are in charge of overseeing the entire staff in the Executive Residence (as the White House is also known).

As chief usher, you are the general manager of the building itself, including construction, maintenance, and remodeling. You manage the staff in charge of feeding the first family and their guests, and also handle the administrative, fiscal, and personnel functions. Your top priority is meeting the first family's needs.

All in a Day's Work

Every morning you meet with the Office of Scheduling and Advance to review the day's events. The rest of the day, an in-house computer provides minute-by-minute updates. The first daughter is running late for a piano lesson? Got it! Time for a veterinarian check-up for the family pet? You're on it!

Not only that, but a tracking system keeps you informed of every member of the family's whereabouts at all times so you know when and where they are in the house. That's how service staffers make beds, nab laundry, dust, vacuum, paint, and make repairs without busting up the family's privacy.

You also tend to the needs of the family's guests. One day it could be a sleepover for the president's son. Another day it could be arranging for an important foreign official and his wife to have dinner with the president and first lady . You work with other staffers to make sure that all guests enjoy their White House visits.

Committed for the Long Haul

So, what's on your agenda for tomorrow? It's time for your monthly meeting with executives from the National Park Service, the Secret Service, the Military Office, and others to go over any repairs, upkeep issues, or security concerns that need attention.

Many jobs at the White House end when presidents leave office. But not the chief usher! You hope to beat the record of your personal role model, Eugene Allen. Mr. Allen served under eight presidents and was the subject for the 2013 movie, *The Butler.*

Your Chief Usher Career Adventure Starts Here

EXPLORE IT!

Use your Internet research skills to find out how long the following former chief ushers served and under which presidents:

Eugene Allen

Irwin "Ike" Hoover

Rex Scouten

Gary Walters

J.B. West

TRY IT!

Don't Complain—Maintain

Look around your bedroom and make a list of anything that needs attention like burnt-out light bulbs, cobwebs in the corners, or a torn bedspread. Offer to help your parents keep your room in good shape. Who knows? You might earn some extra allowance while learning some valuable life skills!

Super-Neat Spreadsheet

Write down a pretend, annual budget for an imaginary mansion. Think about the kinds of work needed to keep it maintained. What kind of staff would you need to help? Then imagine you had a million-dollar annual budget! Where would you divvy the money?

INTELLIGENCE OFFICER

Are you a tech-savvy news junkie? Can you handle complex situations? The U.S. government is in search of an intelligence officer to join its ranks in the White House Situation Room. Must be able to keep secrets at all costs. Fluency in several languages a major plus!

- *Ready to take on this challenge?*
  Turn to page 10.

- *Want to explore a career as the President instead?*
  Go to page 13.

- *Rather consider other choices?*
  Return to page 4.

Check out the CIA Kid Zone at https://www.cia.gov/kids-page.

Situation Station

Down in the west basement of the White House is the Situation Room, which is actually a series of rooms and offices. This is where the president connects with government intelligence agencies in the United States and overseas.

You are one of 30 **intelligence officers** who work in "watch teams" monitoring world events around the clock. Sensors in the ceilings detect cellular signals to prevent **bugging** and unauthorized communication. It is a super secure place where sensitive information is gathered to protect national security.

As the World Turns

In some ways the Situation Room reminds you of a super cool home entertainment center. There are flat-screen television screens all around the room. But those screens aren't tuned into favorite television shows. Instead, each screen represents a watch station for a specific part of the world.

As an intelligence officer monitoring one of these watch stations in the "Sit Room," you prepare several daily reports containing top secret information—and also a lot of charts, graphs, maps, photos, and diagrams—for briefing the president and other important officials on current world events.

Never-Tell Intel

Today when you get to your station you detect a possible **breach** of security and must alert officials at the **Pentagon** right away. So you step into a glass-enclosed phone booth (kind of like Superman when he changes into his cape!) where you can conduct a top secret conversation. You provide essential information to top military officials who decide how to best deal with the problem.

Later in the afternoon, you and some others observe a video feed from **aerial drones** that are surveying military operations in another country. Because the audio is in a foreign language, you use your foreign language skills to interpret for the others. As exciting as the information may be, you can't tell anyone outside your inner intelligence agency circles (even your family and closest BFFs) about what happened. Whatever goes on inside the Situation Room is top-secret, unless government officials decide to release the information to the public. So...shhhhhh.

Your Intelligence Officer Career Adventure Starts Here

EXPLORE IT!

Use your Internet search skills to seek out information about the following:

Images of the Situation Room

History of the Situation Room

Famous briefings in the Situation Room

TRY IT!

Foreign Affairs Expert

An intelligence officer must become an expert in world affairs. To start your training, pick a country or region of the world that interests you. Then go online for a do-it-yourself briefing using the CIA's World Fact Book at www.cia.gov/library/publications/the-world-factbook.

Fluency in a Foreign Language

Intelligence officers often become experts in a specific country or region of the world. That means they must speak and read that country's main language. Choose a foreign language that interests you, and use online resources such as freetranslation.com to teach yourself new words and phrases.

PRESIDENT

Candidate needed to run for the highest office in the land. Seasoned politician, visionary leader, and passionate public speaker preferred. Must get the majority of people in all fifty states to vote for you. Able to withstand intense media scrutiny and withering criticism from all sides. Able to put the nation's best interests above all else.

- *Ready to take on this challenge?*
  Go to page 14.

- *Want to explore a career as Press Secretary instead?*
  Go to page 17.

- *Rather consider other choices?*
  Return to page 4.

Be president for a day at **http://pbskids.org/ democracy/be-president.**

Congratulations!

You just won the presidential election. It took years of planning and campaigning. During your campaign, you visited every state in the union, shook countless hands, and made many important promises. Most importantly, you convinced the majority of American voters to vote for you.

On January 20th, millions of people around the world watched your **inauguration** as you took the oath of office and made an inspiring speech. It's official. You are **president** of the United States of America!

Three Big Jobs

You are in charge of the executive branch of government. That means you are the top boss for 15 enormous government departments and millions of federal employees. One of your first tasks as president is to fill your **Cabinet** with advisors, called secretaries, who will run these departments for you. There is a special room in the White House where you meet regularly with the secretaries of each executive branch department: Agriculture, Commerce, Defense, Education, Energy, Health and Human Services, Homeland Security, Housing and Urban Development, Interior, Labor, State, Transportation, Treasury, and Veterans Affairs.

You are also commander-in-chief of all branches of the military. The Air Force, Army, Coast Guard, Marines, and Navy all answer to you. There will be times when you must make important decisions about sending troops into military conflicts, sending ships into action, and using weapons to defend your nation and its interests in other countries. With people's lives at stake, you do not take this duty lightly.

According to the **U.S. Constitution,** you are also the head of state. In other words, you are the nation's top diplomat and make big decisions about how the U.S. works with other countries. People around the world and their leaders look to you for leadership. When you speak, people listen. So be careful what you say!

Veto Power

There is one thing that you do not do and that is make laws. Only Congress has the power to do that. As president, you do have the right to **veto** laws that you don't like. The legislative process works best when you work together with Congress to do what is best for the people you represent.

Now that you've settled in behind your enormous desk in the Oval Office, it's time to make good on some of those campaign promises...

Your President Career Adventure Starts Here

EXPLORE IT!

Use your Internet research skills to find more about the following:

The three branches of federal government

Your favorite U.S. presidents

The president's Cabinet

TRY IT!

Vote for Me!

Before you can become president, you must get elected first. That means a big national campaign, and no campaign would be complete without bumper stickers. Come up with a clever slogan and cool design for a bumper sticker that is sure to bring out the vote—for you!

My Fellow Americans

It's time for your State of the Union Address. Both houses of Congress, the Supreme Court justices, and all 15 Cabinet secretaries will be gathered at the U.S. Capitol. Millions of Americans will be watching TV and online to hear what you have to say. What will you tell them about your plans for America?

PRESS SECRETARY

Are you a skilled writer who digs politics? Can you meet day-to-day deadlines without breaking a sweat? Would you love to be on a first-name basis with America's most respected politicians and journalists? Top spot open for an articulate and intelligent individual who's not spooked to speak in front of a camera (often televised worldwide!). Be sure to dress for success.

- *Ready to take on this challenge?*
  Turn to page 18.

- *Want to explore a career as a Secret Service Agent instead?*
  Go to page 21.

- *Rather consider other choices?*
  Return to page 4.

See press secretaries at work at **www. whitehousemuseum. org/west-wing/press- secretary.htm**.

Meet the Prez

As the White House **press secretary**, you serve as spokesperson for the U.S. government's current administration and its activities. This means you meet regularly with the president of the United States and other high level officials to get updates on policies, events, and other newsworthy activities.

Because the president is extremely busy running the country, he or she can only grant occasional interviews to professional journalists, who are collectively known as the media. Your job is to speak to the media on the president's behalf, so journalists can relay government-related information to the public.

Meet the Press

You hold weekday press briefings in the James S. Brady Press Briefing Room located inside the White House's West Wing. Most of the journalists present at the daily briefings are members of the White House press corps. The press corps consists of many White House correspondents, who work for various publications, websites, TV news shows, and radio stations.

These news correspondents have been chosen by their employers to work the White House **beat**. Press corps correspondents have assigned seating in the briefing room and also are provided office space in the West Wing, where they can draft their stories before releasing them.

Side Dish

If there's a major event going on, you might also hold a press conference. A press conference is similar to a briefing but is usually more involved. Sometimes the president makes important announcements at press conferences. Press conferences are almost always televised, so you'll be on camera (but don't smile, not if it's news coverage about a serious matter.) You also organize **gaggles**, less formal but on-the-record media gatherings that are held inside your office.

Since you're the press secretary, it's likely that you have a background in political journalism. You and your White House press staff write plenty of press releases to send out news items to the media, but lots of times you're *in* the news. Turn on the national news or pick up the daily newspaper, and you're likely to find a quote from you—so always think before you speak!

Your Press Secretary Career Adventure Starts Here

EXPLORE IT!

Use your Internet search skills to find out more about the following:

Past and present White House press secretaries

White House press releases

White House Briefing Room

TRY IT!

Write a Press Release

Do some research on how to write a press release. There are lots of websites that show the correct format—it needs to include a date, catchy headline, and contact information (in case reporters have further questions about the event). The next time your school or community has big news, write up a press release and let the world know!

Practice Your Interviewing Skills

Grab a friend and a tape recorder, and take turns interviewing each other. Before you hit the "record" button, be sure that you've both drafted a list of intriguing questions. Don't share your questions with your friend, and don't peek at theirs! Find out which of you are skilled at gracefully answering tough questions on the spot.

SECRET SERVICE AGENT

Have a spotless reputation and a spot-on aim? Government in search of strong, silent type to physically protect the President of the United States and other super-important people. Must be willing to work long shifts at oddball hours, sometimes without breaks. Lots of travel required, but very little sightseeing permitted as agents will have to keep their eyes on the prize...er, prez.

- *Ready to take on this challenge?*
  Turn to page 22.

- *Want to explore a career as a Social Secretary instead?*
  Go to page 25.

- *Rather consider other choices?*
  Return to page 4.

Learn more about the history of the Secret Service at **www. secretservice.gov/about/ history/events**.

Join the Elite? Sweet!

Your job as a **Secret Service agent** is to protect current and former presidents, their families, and other high level officials. Before your assignment with the Presidential Protective Division, you proved yourself by working with Secret Service's Investigative Support Division. That's where you did some serious detective work investigating money-related crimes— **counterfeiting**, **money laundering**, and more!

To Serve and Protect

Now you have earned the plum assignment of working as part of the president's security detail! That means you'll, literally, rub elbows with the U.S. President. But don't get too stoked—you're not his or her friend, or even an advisor. Your job is strictly to protect the president from physical harm, and you're expected, for the most part, to keep your lips zipped...on and off duty.

As you spend lots of up-close time with the president, you balance being totally alert for any potential threats to his or her safety, while basically pretending to be invisible while he or she goes about the business of running the country. You hear a lot of inside info about politics as well as the president's personal life but, as the saying goes, what happens at the White House stays at the White House! You are sworn to secrecy.

Shift or Shaft?

You rotate around-the-clock shifts with other special agents. Tonight you're working the midnight shift out of state, keeping watch outside the back entrance of a mansion, where the president and first lady are staying overnight with friends. You keep a keen eye on your surroundings, not leaving your post until your replacement arrives.

At the crack of dawn, the president steps outside in his athletic gear for an early-morning jog. He runs the perimeter of the large estate's lush grounds, and you keep pace alongside him the whole course—armed with a loaded pistol and other protective gear.

After fellow agents check on details for the president's motorcade back to the airport, your shift ends. You return to Air Force One for a good day's rest before another shift begins at the White House.

You take your job very seriously. After all, there are people who would do the president harm if they got the chance. You don't intend for that to happen. Not on your watch! You are well-trained, dedicated, and ready to take a bullet for the president, if necessary.

Your Secret Service Agent Career Adventure Starts Here

EXPLORE IT!

Use your Internet search skills to find out more about the following:

History of the U.S. Secret Service

The presidential car (also known as the "beast")

Presidential assassinations

TRY IT!

Apply Yourself

Go to http://www.secretservice.gov/join/apply/ to see what it takes to score a spot with the Secret Service! Find out what's expected from you during the job interview, figure out which documents you need to present, and download a study guide for the entrance exam. Draft a pretend resume that includes your educational and career goals.

Pay Attention

Secret Service agents are trained to pay attention to details. That way they can instantly respond when anything is amiss. Try staring at a photograph or picture in a book. Then turn the image over and write down as many details about it as you can remember. Take another look at the picture and see how you did. Secret Service standard-issue sunglasses not required.

SOCIAL SECRETARY

Special Invitation

Do you throw parties everyone talks about all year long? Currently in search of the ultimate event planner to organize White House social gatherings. Tea for two or formal dinner for two hundred? You can take it in stride! Ideal candidate has impeccable taste and social graces, and is not skittish about entertaining the rich and famous.

- *Ready to take on this challenge?*
  Turn to page 26.

- *Want to explore a career as a Chief Usher instead?*
  Go to page 5.

- *Rather consider other choices?*
  Return to page 4.

Get the social scoop at www.whitehousehistory.org/the-white-house-social-secretary-job-description-and-work-culture.

Party with Panache

Fancy invites? Check! Delectable menu? Check! Decorations that wow? Check! You thoughtfully choose the paper, lettering, and wording for the invitations. The food that's served is a carefully planned menu you create with the president's chef. Before deciding on the perfect décor, you chat with the first lady to get her ideas and input.

As **social secretary**, you're in charge of every social gathering attended by the president, first family, and other senior political staffers. Where do you get to do all of this high-falutin' party planning? The White House Social Office is located in the East Wing of the White House where, according to tradition, you work closely with the president's spouse. There you manage and coordinate all sorts of events. Some are political. Some are just for fun like the annual White House Easter Egg Roll!

First Things First

The very first event you get to plan? A luncheon to honor...you! It's a White House tradition for each incoming social secretary to host a gathering of former social secretaries, who attend to welcome you to the position and give you some insider scoop on how to best step into your new post.

Social Standing

Up next? The President is hosting an official **state dinner** for a foreign **prime minister** and 150 **dignitaries**. You need this event to go off without a hitch or a glitch. This work is way more important than being a wedding planner since **diplomatic ties** are at stake! Besides choosing invitations, centerpieces, lighting, and a five-course meal, you consult with the U.S. Department of State to help you draft a guest list and organize seating arrangements, very deliberately choosing who sits next to whom.

Guests include **heads of state**, important politicians, high-profile foreigners, military leaders, respected professors, famous authors, accomplished athletes, A-list celebrities, and more. You want to have live music, so will you book a solo pop singer to perform or go all-out with an entire classical orchestra? It's your call!

Oh, and do you get to attend the event you poured your heart into planning? Not always…but sometimes!

Your Social Secretary Career Adventure Starts Here

EXPLORE IT!

Do some research to find out why the White House Social Secretary might have to meet with the following people:

*Chief of **Protocol** of the United States*

White House Chief Usher

Uniformed military aides

TRY IT!

Map Out a Plan

Pretend you're planning a party at the White House for any occasion you choose. Grab a notebook and pen, and list all the details of your event. Who's invited? What are you serving? Is it held indoors or out on the lawn? What activities are you hosting? Will there be entertainment—your favorite pop star perhaps?

Write an Invite

Now that you've planned your event (see above), design a fake invitation for it. Break out some construction paper, colored markers, glitter, and other art supplies, and create something extravagant. Don't forget to include all the nitty-gritty party details!

WRITE YOUR OWN CAREER ADVENTURE

WRITE YOUR OWN CAREER ADVENTURE

You just read about six awesome White House careers:

- Chief usher
- Intelligence officer
- President

- Press secretary
- Secret Service agent
- Social secretary

Which is your favorite? Pick one, and imagine what it would be like to do that job. Now write your own career adventure!

_____

_____

_____

_____

_____

_____

_____

_____

Go online to download free activity sheets at www.cherrylakepublishing.com/activities.

ATTENTION, ADVENTURERS! Please do NOT write in this book if it is not yours. Use a separate piece of paper.

GLOSSARY

aerial drone a small unmanned vehicle that is essentially a flying robot, often used for videography

Air Force One aircraft specifically designed, built, and used for the purpose of transporting the president of the United States

beat specialized reporting on a particular subject, issue, location, organization, or sector

breach failure to observe a code of conduct

bugging concealing miniature audio equipment to secretly record conversations

Cabinet a body of advisers to the U.S. president, composed of the heads of the executive departments of the government

chief usher head of household staff and operations at the White House

counterfeiting the practice of manufacturing fake replicas of something, often money

dignitary important person due to high rank or office

diplomatic ties international relations between countries

gaggle an informal news briefing that is not videotaped but is recorded by written transcripts

head of state the chief representative of a country, such as a president or other governmental leader

inauguration ceremony to mark the beginning of a new president's formal admission to office.

intelligence officer person charged with obtaining intelligence, or information, especially for use by the president and other high level officials

money laundering the process for concealing illegally obtained money

on-the-record officially noted as it pertains to a statement that is available to the general public and not held in confidentiality

Pentagon headquarters of the U.S. Department of Defense

president the elected head of a republican state

press secretary person whose job is to give information about an important or famous person or organization to news reporters

prime minister the head of the executive branch of a government

Secret Service agent person responsible for protecting presidents and their families, presidential candidates, and foreign dignitaries visiting the United States

social secretary a person who arranges the social activities of a person or organization

state dinner a banquet hosted by the U.S. government to honor a foreign leader

U.S. Constitution document drafted by America's founding fathers that embodies the fundamental laws and principles by which the United States is governed

veto constitutional right to reject a decision or proposal made by a law-making body

INDEX

ABOUT THE AUTHORS

Diane Lindsey Reeves is the author of lots of children's books. She lives in Cary, North Carolina, and her favorite thing to do is play with her grandkids—Conrad, Evan, Reid, and Hollis Grace.

Kelly Anne White is author of *The Bible Adventure Book of Scavenger Hunts* (HealthyLearning.com), as well as the upcoming *Jesus Groupie* series of books. Kelly is a book-manuscript editor for Kirkus Media and former freelance contributor for HarperCollins Christian Publishing. Prior to her focus on book publishing, Kelly spent 15 years near the tippy-top of the masthead of Girls' Life magazine as its senior executive editor. Kelly lives joyfully in Baltimore, Maryland, and she loves her career as a book author!